D1710184

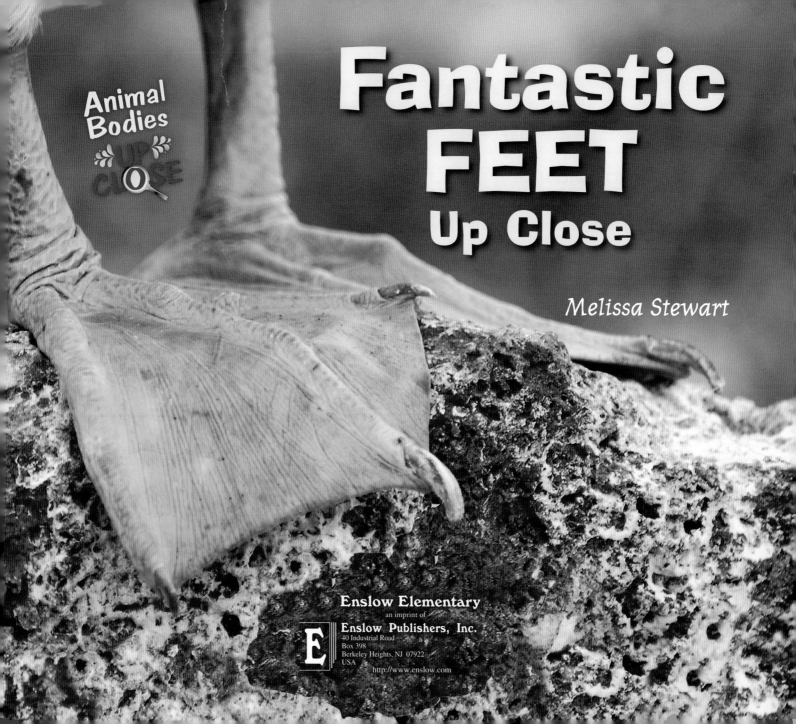

Animal
Bodies
UP
CLOSE

Fantastic
FEET
Up Close

Melissa Stewart

Enslow Elementary
an imprint of
E **Enslow Publishers, Inc.**
40 Industrial Road
Box 398
Berkeley Heights, NJ 07922
USA
http://www.enslow.com

CONTENTS

WORDS TO KNOW

hooves (HOOVZ)—The hard, thick feet of horses and some other animals.

parachute (PAER uh shoot)—A large cloth that helps a person or a package float down slowly from the sky.

stride (STRIHD)—A long step.

strut (STRUHT)—To walk in a way that shows other people you think you are important.

3

FLYING FROG

Animals use their feet in all kinds of ways. This frog has huge feet. They act like a **parachute** as the frog falls from a tree in the forest. They also help the frog land with a gentle plop. What a great trick!

CAMEL

What has feet as big as a dinner plate but only two toes? A camel does. As it walks, its toes spread wide. That way the camel does not sink into the sand.

SEA STAR

A sea star has hundreds of tiny feet. They are on the bottom of each arm. The feet hold on tight to rocks. They also help the sea star move from place to place.

BLUE-FOOTED BOOBY

UP CLOSE

How does this bird attract a mate? He dances. He spreads his wings wide and whistles. Then he **struts**, slides, shuffles, and stomps his bright blue feet. What a show!

Webbed feet are good for swimming too. They help the bird paddle through the water.

GECKO

A gecko has many enemies.
But it can stay safe by darting up
and down trees. It can zip across
branches, too. It can even walk on ceilings.
How can a gecko do all that? Its feet have millions
of hairs. They can grab onto all kinds of surfaces.
They can even hold onto glass.

HORSE

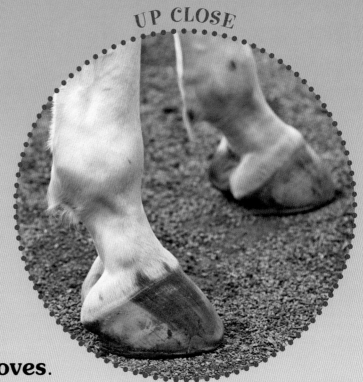

A horse's feet are called **hooves**.
They look like the horse's big, thick
toenails. A horse runs on its tiptoes, so it can
stretch farther than other animals with each
stride. That's one reason why a horse is so fast.

AARDVARK

An aardvark (AHRD vahrk) is the fastest digger on Earth. Its feet have long claws. Each claw is shaped like a shovel. An aardvark's feet are perfect for digging up ants and termites to eat.

UP CLOSE

YOUR FEET

You are an animal, too.
You have two feet. They take you
anywhere you want to go.

You take about eight thousand steps
every day. In your life, you'll walk far enough
to circle Earth four and a half times!

GUESSING GAME

1. **How many feet do most centipedes have?** A. **0**

2. **How many feet do earthworms have?** B. **1**

3. **How many feet do millipedes have?** C. **around 50**

4. **How many feet do snails have?** D. **up to 400**

(Write your answers on a piece of paper. Please do not write in this book!)

See answers on page 24.

centipede

earthworm

millipede

snail

21

LEARN MORE

Books

Bozzo, Linda. *Amazing Animal Feet*. New York: PowerKids Press, 2008.

Hall, Peg. *Whose Feet Are These?* Mankato, Minn.: Picture Window Books, 2006.

Jenkins, Steve and Robin Page. *What Do You Do With a Tail Like This?* Boston: Houghton Mifflin, 2008.

Leake, Diyan. *Feet*. Chicago: Heinemann-Raintree, 2007.

WEB SITES

Environmental Education for Kids: EEK! Track Quick for Beginners
<http://dnr.wi.gov/org/caer/
ce/eek/cool/
trackQuizLVLOne.htm>

Observing Animals' Feet
http://www.brandywinezoo.org/
games/animal_feet.pdf

INDEX

A
aardvark, 16

B
blue-footed
booby, 10

C
camel, 6

F
flying frog, 4

G
gecko, 12

H
hooves, 14
horse, 14
human feet, 18

P
parachute, 4

S
sea star, 8
stride, 14
strut, 10

Note to Parents and Teachers: The Animal Bodies Up Close series supports the National Science Education Standards for K–4 science. The Words to Know section introduces subject-specific vocabulary words, including pronunciation and definitions. Early readers may need help with these new words.

Enslow Elementary, an imprint of Enslow Publishers, Inc.

Enslow Elementary® is a registered trademark of Enslow Publishers, Inc.

Copyright © 2012 by Melissa Stewart

All rights reserved.

No part of this book may be reproduced by any means without the written permission of the publisher.

Library of Congress Cataloging-in-Publication Data

Stewart, Melissa.
  Fantastic feet up close / Melissa Stewart.
    p. cm. — (Animal bodies up close)
  Includes index.
  Summary: "Discover how different animals use their feet to move, hunt, and stay safe"— Provided by publisher.
  ISBN 978-0-7660-3890-5
  1. Foot—Juvenile literature. I. Title.
  QL950.7.S738 2011
  591.47'9—dc22
                          2011003337

Future editions:
Paperback ISBN 978-1-4644-0084-1
ePUB ISBN 978-1-4645-0991-9
PDF ISBN 978-1-4645-0991-6

Printed in China

012012 Leo Paper Group, Heshan City, Guangdong, China

10 9 8 7 6 5 4 3 2 1

To Our Readers: We have done our best to make sure all Internet Addresses in this book were active and appropriate when we went to press. However, the author and the publisher have no control over and assume no liability for the material available on those Internet sites or on other Web sites they may link to. Any comments or suggestions can be sent by e-mail to comments@enslow.com or to the address on the back cover.

Photo Credits: © 2011 Photos.com, a division of Getty Images, pp. 3 (parachute), 18, 19; ©Abpl Image Library/Animals Animals, p. 17; © blickwinkel/Alamy, p. 4; iStockphoto.com: © Charles Gibson, p. 6, © Hedda Gjerpen, p. 14, © jeridu, p. 21 (centipede), © John Shepherd, p. 21 (earthworm), © Roger de Montfort, p. 10; OSF/Photolibrary, p. 12; Photo Researchers, Inc.: Nigel J. Dennis, p. 16, Philippe Psaila, pp. 13, 23, Stephen Dalton p. 5; Shutterstock.com, pp. 1, 2, 3 (hooves, stride, strut), 8, 9, 15, 21 (millipede, snail); © Studio Carlo Dani/Animals Animals/Earth Scenes, p. 7; Tui De Roy/Minden Pictures, p. 11.

Cover Photos: Shutterstock.com

Series Literacy Consultant:
Allan A. De Fina, PhD
Dean, College of Education
Professor of Literacy Education
New Jersey City University
Past President of the New Jersey Reading
  Association

Science Consultant:
Helen Hess, PhD
Professor of Biology
College of the Atlantic
Bar Harbor, Maine

Answers to the Guessing Game

Centipedes: C. around 50	Millipedes: D. up to 400
Earthworms: A. 0	Snails: B. 1